Date: 2/7/14

SPACE COWBOY CALEB
AND THE NIGHT SKY ROUND-UP

BY TINA DYBVIK • ILLUSTRATED BY ADAM RECORD

LEARNING ABOUT THE NIGHT SKY

PICTURE WINDOW BOOKS
a capstone imprint

One late summer night, Caleb and Jackie camped beneath the stars. Caleb woke and looked out of the tent to see a vast stardust road stretching into the sky. He wanted to be a cowboy, and this looked like the ride of a lifetime!

Caleb rubbed his eyes. He shook Jackie awake. "Let's saddle up!" he said. "The meteor shower is tonight. Let's take the stardust road to get a closer look."

"Stardust road?" Jackie asked.

"COME ON!" Caleb yelled. **"THE NIGHT SKY AWAITS!"**

NEIGH!

A meteor is a piece of metal or rock that falls from space. It burns brightly as it passes through the Earth's atmosphere. A meteor shower happens when lots of meteors fall from one direction of the sky.

The two friends jumped onto Rocket and rode to the ridge. They stopped to gaze at the moon.

"The moon is so small tonight. It looks like my thumbnail," Jackie said.

"It's a crescent," said Caleb. "It's the phase when the moon looks smallest."

"Phase?" repeated Jackie.

"Yep," said Caleb. "Crescent, quarter, gibbous, and full are phases of the moon."

He opened his notepad to draw.

"The sun shines on the moon, making it glow with reflected light," Caleb said.

The moon circles Earth every 29.53 days. During that time, the moon goes through all of its phases. Sunlight strikes half the moon's surface. The moon phase we see from Earth depends on where the moon is compared to the sun and Earth.

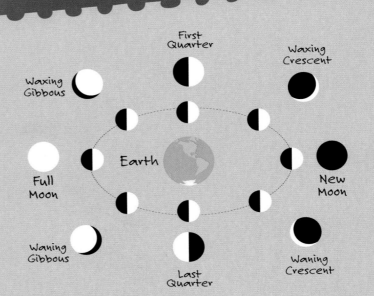

First Quarter

Waxing Crescent

Waxing Gibbous

Sunlight

Earth

Full Moon

New Moon

Waning Gibbous

Last Quarter

Waning Crescent

"What's next?" asked Jackie.

"We have to find northeast. The August meteors come from there," answered Caleb.

"Do you have a compass?" Jackie asked.

"We can use the stars to find direction! Dad taught me to spot Polaris," said Caleb. "That's another name for the North Star."

"So Polaris is north," said Jackie. "But where do we start looking?"

LITTLE DIPPER

NORTH STAR

BIG DIPPER

The Big Dipper is a group of seven stars called an asterism. The stars are part of a constellation called Ursa Major, or Great Bear. It can be seen in the night sky year-round in the northern hemisphere.

"We can use the Big Dipper as a guide. The two outer stars of the dipper point right to Polaris."

"Let's find those meteors," Caleb said. **"YAH! UP INTO THE SKY WE GO!"**

Rocket rode hard into the darkness. He didn't stop until they were in outer space and the Big Dipper was right in front of them.

SLURP!

SLURP!

"Whoa!" said Caleb. "Good boy, Rocket! You must need a drink."

The horse was tired from the climb. He drank long and deep from the dipper bowl.

"Now that we found the Big Dipper, let's see if we can catch a meteoroid!" Caleb said twirling his rope.

"How do we find one?" asked Jackie. As he spoke, something zoomed across the sky.

"JEEPERS!" shouted Jackie. **"WHAT'S THAT?"**

Caleb laughed. "That's a meteoroid! Once it gets close to Earth, it will start burning brightly. Then we'd call it a meteor or a shooting star."

Caleb threw his rope toward the meteoroid. "Got it!" he yelled.

"COOL! LET'S PULL IT THIS WAY," said Jackie.

Caleb and Jackie pulled on the rope until the meteoroid was close enough to touch. Jackie pulled out his pickax and began chipping away.

Jackie held up the rock he had chipped off. "You can let that meteoroid go now," he said.

Caleb loosened his rope, and the meteoroid slipped through the loop. "Can I see that piece?" Caleb asked.

Jackie held up the rock for Caleb to see.

"It looks like there are shiny flecks in it," said Caleb. "Most meteoroids have some metal in them."

If a meteor survives its fall to the ground, it is called a meteorite. People all around the world find meteorites. Many meteorites have iron and nickel in them.

Jackie wound up. He pitched the piece of meteoroid.

It skipped back onto its path. "Look at it go!" he called.

"Let's move on," said Caleb. "There's a lot of sky to see."

The friends and Rocket continued on the stardust road. Before long, they were dodging satellites.

"What are these things?" asked Jackie. "They look like they have wings!"

"They're satellites."

"Like TV satellites?" Jackie asked.

"Or for cell phones, or GPS," Caleb said. "We better get out of here. There are thousands of satellites up here."

"Let's ride!" shouted Jackie.

"Yeehaw!" said Caleb. They held on tight as Rocket galloped away.

CLIP-CLOP!

CLIP-CLOP!

CLIP-CLOP!

Satellites are machines that circle Earth in space. They track the weather and send information to radios, TVs, cell phones, and GPS map systems. If you look up on a dark night, you might see a satellite moving steadily across the sky.

LEFT ON 1-80

11:18   200

800-123-4567

1	2	3
4	5	6
7	8	9
*	0	#

When they were far away from the satellites, they rested. Earth was a big blue ball in space.

"What a view!" said Jackie.

"It's beautiful," Caleb agreed. "You know, we should be able to see other planets from up here too."

"Really?" asked Jackie.

"Venus is the closest planet to Earth," Caleb replied. He opened his notepad to draw again. "See that steady light by the sun?"

"Well, hello Venus!" said Jackie.

VENUS

SUN

Venus is covered in a thick blanket of moving clouds. The sun reflects off of these clouds. From Earth, Venus appears to be shining. But its "light" is really the reflection of sunlight.

"We should get back to the farm," said Caleb as he steered Rocket back toward Earth.

The two friends followed the stardust road until a wall of light blocked their way.

"It's the aurora borealis," said Caleb. "You know, the northern lights."

"WOW, IT'S BRIGHT!" said Jackie. "I bet we can jump over it. Rocket is a great jumper!"

"Not with the two of us riding."

Caleb looked for another way. There was only one road leading back to the farm. He was about to give up, when he saw a flash. The fireball streaked across the sky. Caleb tossed his rope toward the meteor's tail. **"GOT IT!"** he yelled.

"Nice roping!" yelled Jackie.

"GIDDYAP!" shouted Caleb. And over the aurora they went, pulled by the meteor as it traveled toward Earth.

AURORA BOREALIS

Auroras are colorful bands of light that appear in the northern and southern skies, often far north or south of the equator. They appear when wind and particles from the sun hit the magnetic field that surrounds Earth.

As Rocket trotted slowly to the farm below, the stardust road faded behind them. They were back on the farm. Caleb and Jackie headed for the tent.

NEIGH!

"Maybe I should be an astronaut instead of a cowboy," said Caleb.

Jackie smiled. **"YOU'LL BE SPACE COWBOY CALEB!"**

They fell asleep and dreamed of roping the moon.

HEADS UP! IT'S A METEOR SHOWER

You don't need a telescope to see a meteor shower. You can spot them with just your eyes!

What you do:

- Find a dark place away from lights with no trees or buildings blocking the sky.
- Dress warm—layers are good.
- Lie down on a blanket.
- Look up and watch the wide night sky.

Tips:

- The best viewing is late at night.
- A bright moon can make the meteors hard to see.
- Give your eyes time to adjust to the dark.

Here's a list of dates and names for the largest meteor showers:

- Jan 2-3 Quadrantids
- Apr 22-23 Lyrids
- May 5-6 Eta Aquarids
- Jul 29-30 Delta Aquarids
- Aug 11-12 Perseids
- Oct 21-22 Orionids
- Nov 4-5 Taurids
- Nov 16-17 Leonids
- Dec 12-13 Geminids
- Dec 22-23 Ursids

GLOSSARY

atmosphere—the mixture of gases that surrounds Earth

compass—an instrument used for finding directions

constellation—a group of stars that forms a shape

crescent—a curved shape that looks like the moon when it is mostly in shadow and only a sliver of it is visible in the sky

gibbous—when the lit part of the moon looks larger than half of a circle and smaller than a full circle

GPS (global positioning system)—a computer that receives signals from satellites in space; a GPS is used to find the location of an object

magnetic field—a line of force that pushes or pulls moving particles

meteor—a piece of rock that burns up as it passes through Earth's atmosphere

meteorite—a piece of meteor that falls all the way to the ground

meteoroid—a piece of rock that broke off a comet or asteroid and is floating in space

phase—a stage; the moon's phases are the different shapes it appears to take during 29.53 days

READ MORE

Hughes, Catherine D. *First Big Book of Space.* National Geographic Little Kids. Washington, D.C.: National Geographic, 2012.

Meister, Cari. *The Story of Ursa Major and Ursa Minor: A Roman Constellation Myth*. Night Sky Stories. Mankato, Minn.: Capstone, 2013.

Mist, Rosalind. *Asteroids, Comets, and Meteors.* Up in Space. Mankato, Minn.: QEB Pub., 2013.

INDEX

INTERNET SITES

FactHound offers a safe, fun way to find Internet sites related to this book. All of the sites on FactHound have been researched by our staff.

Here's all you do:

Visit *www.facthound.com*

Type in this code: 9781404883178

Super-cool stuff! Check out projects, games and lots more at www.capstonekids.com

Thanks to our advisers for their expertise, research, and advice:

Susan Lepri, PhD, Associate Research Scientist
Atmospheric, Ocean, and Space Sciences
The University of Michigan

Terry Flaherty, PhD, Professor of English
Minnesota State University, Mankato

Editor: Shelly Lyons
Designer: Alison Thiele
Art Director: Nathan Gassman
Production Specialist: Jennifer Walker
The illustrations in this book were created digitally.

Picture Window Books are published by Capstone,
1710 Roe Crest Drive, North Mankato, Minnesota 56003
www.capstonepub.com

Library of Congress Cataloging-in-Publication Data
Dybvik, Tina.
Space Cowboy Caleb and the night sky round-up : learning about the night sky / by Tina Dybvik ; illustrated by Adam Record.
p. cm. — (Take it outside)
Audience: K-3.
Summary: "Through the fantastical story of a young boy, text and illustrations introduce features of the night sky, such as stars, meteors, and phases of the moon"—Provided by publisher.
ISBN 978-1-4048-8317-8 (library binding)
ISBN 978-1-4795-1938-5 (paperback)
ISBN 978-1-4795-1903-3 (eBook pdf)
1. Astronomy—Juvenile literature. 2. Meteors—Juvenile literature. I. Record, Adam, ill. II. Title.
QB46.D93 2014
520—dc23

Printed in the United States of America in
Stevens Point, Wisconsin.
032013   007227WZF13

LOOK FOR ALL THE BOOKS IN THE TAKE IT OUTSIDE SERIES:

KIT AND MATEO **JOURNEY** INTO THE **CLOUDS**
LEARNING ABOUT CLOUDS

THE LOST TREASURE OF **LARRY LONGFOOT**
LEARNING TO USE A MAP

SADIE'S SEED ADVENTURES
LEARNING ABOUT SEEDS

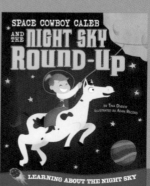

SPACE COWBOY CALEB AND THE **NIGHT SKY ROUND-UP**
LEARNING ABOUT THE NIGHT SKY